The

Exploring the Spiritual Truth at the

Heart of the World's Religions

The Journey

Exploring the Spiritual Truth at the
Heart of the World's Religions

Luke Eastwood

MOON
BOOKS

Winchester, UK
Washington, USA

First published by Moon Books, 2012
Moon Books is an imprint of John Hunt Publishing Ltd., Laurel House,
Station Approach, Alresford, Hants, SO24 9JH, UK
office1@jhpbooks.net
www.johnhuntpublishing.com
www.moon-books.net

For distributor details and how to order please visit the 'Ordering' section on
our website.

Text copyright: Luke Eastwood 2012

ISBN: 978 1 84694 014 9

A CIP catalogue record for this book is available from the British Library.

Design: Stuart Davies

Printed and bound by CPI Group (UK) Ltd, Croydon, CR0 4YY

CONTENTS

The publishers wish to make acknowledgement of the following for granting permission to use copyright material: Faber & Faber Ltd for an extract from 'Little Gidding' from *Four Quartets* by T.S. Eliot.

A big thank you to all my family and friends for all their love and support, and also many thanks to all the staff at Moon Books.

Preface to Second Edition

This collection brings together some of my writings on spirituality in one volume. The original edition was previously published in Ireland only under the pseudonym Joseph Dawton, in 2005. At the time I considered the message of the book to be far more important than the writer, although this still holds true I no longer feel the need to conceal my identity.

Whereas most of my other published work concentrates on Celtic spirituality, namely the Druidic path, this work has a far wider focus. At this time the world is still embroiled in religious and cultural conflict while we head ever closer to oblivion. Whilst we continue to argue over minutiae, we continue to miss the whole point of religiosity or spirituality – i.e. the process of becoming closer to and more like the divine.

Truly mankind is unique on this planet in being fully cognisant of our predicament, possessing free will and the ability to consciously change the course of our evolution. I am by no means the first to give a dire warning of our hubris, indeed such a message can be detected in *The Epic of Gilgamesh*, written thousands of years ago and perhaps the oldest known book of its kind.

What is different now is that on many levels the evidence is mounting of our rapidly approaching the end of the road. Those of any wisdom at all can see that our hedonist ideology, our destructive method of living, our increasing selfishness and the general lack of concern is a far greater danger than any predator, natural phenomenon or other theoretical enemy. For those who are aware of our self-defeating actions the problem has been to precipitate change in a human world that is resistant to ideas and behaviours that challenge self-gratification.

Lack of belief in the divine, a higher purpose and morality as a general principle is destined to destroy us if we are unable to find a way of transcending both our detached state and the careless way in which we treat each other and the world around us.

The destruction of mankind or the 'end of the world' has been predicted for millennia and thus far we have survived the rise and fall of empires, great plagues, famines and war. However, we now live in a time when the technology that we have created has the power to destroy us. The most obvious example is the thermonuclear bomb. However, far less visible threats of our own devising look more likely to destroy.

Our (western) model for living, which has taken hold all over the world, is so detrimental to all life that I can only see death for humanity if there is not a rapid and complete abandonment of this model. Apart from the violence, savage inequality and wastage, we are slowly poisoning the entire planet and ourselves for short-sighted goals such as profit.

The enlightened ones of the past have been very clear to

highlight the folly of making money and material possessions our gods. It is from the last two hundred years that we finally see the repercussions of such a self-destructive obsession. What use will money and wealth be to those who possess them when the rivers and the land are poisoned, the seas devoid of life and the air polluted beyond tolerance?

On an instinctive level, if not a conscious or intellectual one, I believe that most of us know that we are headed in the wrong direction. It is true that recognition of our problems has increased, but this is no more than mildly slowing the acceleration of a juggernaut that is hurtling at great speed towards an abyss. This metaphysical discomfort desperately needs to instigate not just a spiritual awakening of the heart and mind, but an irreversible transformation in how we live.

This book does not contain any practical solutions to our physical problems, but it does try to attend to the spiritual and moral distemper that is the cause of all the chaos and destruction that we manifest. A dry intellectual understanding of our mistakes is not going to save us. True and lasting change will only come if we feel and know that we are wrong on a soul level. Only when we truly see, believe and understand the error of our ways can we begin to change in any meaningful way.

The prophets of the past did not recommend virtue and spiritual living because they were kill-joys, they knew that ultimately that is the only way for us to survive. We have been divinely gifted with the ability to choose; while there is still time let us choose the path of love, integrity and life.

Luke Eastwood, May 2012.

Introduction

The core teachings of Jesus, Muhammad, Moses, Buddha, Lao Tzu or any of those who were enlightened are exactly the same – they are about the nature of man, the nature of the universe and the nature of God.

How is it then that we can have ignored so much of the gifts of wisdom that they brought to us? How can countless generations have fought over what are essentially the same beliefs? The answer to that question has puzzled mankind for almost as long as wars have been fought, and maybe no sufficient answer can be found. Regardless of why we have failed to understand one another's view, we must continue to search for unity of understanding if there is to be any hope for mankind.

Priests of all faiths continue to shout at us of the evil of our ways, our failure to adhere to the codes and doctrines laid down and they decry the heresy of other sects and other religions. Perhaps it is those who would be our spiritual masters who have lost their way and can no longer impart the wisdom with which they have supposedly been entrusted.

The purpose of this book is not to divide but to show the unity of belief that exists in the world. I believe that we are at a point in human history that if we cannot re-evaluate our relationship with our fellow man, with our environment and with God we will perish.

The path has been clearly marked for us and re-drawn many times, yet collectively we choose to ignore what is staring us in the face. It does not matter which book of God you pick up, the answers to all the eternal questions are there if you have eyes to see them. All that we will ever need to know is here and has always been present within the hidden depths of our hearts, if this little book can lead one person to see this then my time has not been wasted.

Note: Where I have used words such as God, man, mankind etc it is intended to cover both genders and they are used simply for brevity and convenience.

Part i
The Hidden Path

The Garden

Once there was a garden and that garden was the world. Mankind lived in that garden in happy ignorance, until one day people ate of the tree of knowledge. As they ate the fruit of the tree of knowledge, the tree of life vanished before them, never to be seen again, and the garden became just an ordinary place...

It became a place to be divided into parcels, bought and sold, built upon and fought over until every wilderness was swallowed up. Those men who had not eaten the fruit of the tree of knowledge either yielded to the others or perished at their hands – and thus gradually mankind swept through the world, ever increasing in both knowledge and number.

As men's knowledge grew, so too did their desire until all was refashioned by it and the world shone nightly with the lights of vast cities, the forests gave way to endless fields and every creature of land and sea was allowed live only to serve man's insatiable needs.

The gods looked down upon their children and said of us 'What have you done to your home?' Their sighs became the howling whirlwinds that uproot both tree and dwelling. Their bitter tears swelled the rivers and oceans until they broke upon the land leaving disaster in their wake. The heat of their fury baked the earth so that lakes emptied and rich pasture turned to desert sand.

But even in their fury, the gods still took pity upon mankind, as it is easy to forgive the foolishness of children. And so, in their mercy, they allowed men, for one last time, the chance to amend their ways... and that time is NOW.

The One True Path

Many paths lead to the divine. There is but one God although he/she is known by many names and faces. When mankind crawled from the belly of the earth, struggling for consciousness was not God God, as now and for all time? It is not God who has changed but mankind.

As no two lives and no two men are the same, the expression and experience of God is as infinite as time itself. All the great prophets and sages down the ages knew this, it is not mankind who defines what God is, it is God who lives through us and all existence and God who defines us.

It is our greatest folly that we seek to know the unknowable, to follow the one true path, and in doing so it has torn mankind apart and led us further away from that which we most desire.

The supreme science is to know nothing.
Johann Valentin Andreae

There is one road that none may travel but thou alone.
Anon

It is you who must make the effort.
The great of the past only show the way.
Those who think and follow the path
become free of the bondage of mara.
Gautama Siddhartha (Buddha)

Giving

It is a common adage that it is better to give than to receive. However, many do not truly believe this.

It is a paradox that in giving we receive more than we could ever hope to by hoarding gifts. Is it not true that the more love we give the deeper grows the well of love within us?

One cannot run out of love except by refusing to give it.

If you have money don't lend it at interest.
Rather give it to someone from whom you won't get it back.
Yeshua Ben Miriam (Jesus of Nazareth)

Woe to those who pray but are heedless in their prayer;
who make a show of piety and give no alms to the destitute.
Muhammad

He who acts after giving up all desire, who is free
from any sort of 'mineness' or egoism, he alone attains
tranquillity.
From The Bhagavad-Gítá

Time

Time is a concept unique to man, as far as we know no other creatures on this earth care for it, if they are even aware of it. We live our lives obsessed by the passing of time, looking to regain the past or discover our future rather than living in the moment that is now.

Our time here is so brief, the age of men is as nothing when compared to all the ages of the earth, from its creation over four billion years ago. A single human life is but a drop in the ocean of time, even the life of the earth is little more than that when compared to the immeasurable vastness of time.

The Universe is a lodging house for the myriad things
And time itself is a travelling guest of the centuries.
This floating life is like a dream.
How often can one enjoy oneself?
Li Bai

There was a water-drop, it joined the sea,
A speck of dust, it was fused with earth;
What of your entering and leaving this world?
A fly appeared, and disappeared.
Omar Khayyam

Knowledge

A person can spend his or her life studying philosophy, religion, science, art and all aspects of the human condition and yet at the end of it all still not know what lies within their own heart.

To apply knowledge without wisdom and understanding is as pointless as to battle the wind with a sword.

We shall not cease from exploration
And the end of all our exploring
Will be to arrive where we started
And know the place for the first time.
T. S. Eliot

If during the whole of his life a fool lives with a wise man,
he never knows the path of wisdom as the spoon never
knows the taste of soup.
Gautama Siddhartha (Buddha)

Mankind and Nature

In Genesis (from the Pentateuch or Old Testament) it states that mankind was created in God's image and that we have dominion over the earth. Mankind in his arrogance took the literal meaning of this as truth, failing to see that the story of Genesis is an analogy.

All things are created in God's image and if we have dominion over the earth that surely means that we are its custodians and we have a responsibility to protect it – it is not ours to rape and pillage.

This we know: all things are connected,
like the blood which unites one family.
Whatever befalls the earth
befalls the sons of the earth,
man did not weave the web of life –
he is simply one strand in it.
Whatever he does to the web
he does to himself.
Seatlh, Suquamish Chief

The best of men is only a man at best.
Kit Williams

Does one measure by the hollow of a human hand
the waters of the great ocean?
Are the heavens estimated by the span of fingers?
In one 1/3 of a measure can any contain
the dust of the earth,
And weigh the mountains in a balance
or the hills in scales?
Man did not make these.
How can he measure the spirit of God?
Dead Sea Scroll 4Q511

The Spiritual Path

The spiritual path is long, narrow and arduous; often our destination is beyond sight and our task seems hopeless.

Never give up, to follow the path is as important as reaching your destination, even a snail will arrive where it is going eventually.

Faith is taking the first step, even when you don't see the whole staircase.
Martin Luther King Jr.

Neither father, sons nor one's relations can stop the King of Death.
When he comes with all his power a man's relations cannot save him.
A man who is virtuous and wise understands the meaning of this
And swiftly strives with all his might to clear a path to Nirvana.
Gautama Siddhartha (Buddha)

Enter by the narrow gate.
The path that leads to destruction is wide and easy.
Many follow it. But the narrow gate and hard road lead to life, few discover it.
Yeshua Ben Miriam (Jesus of Nazareth)

Joy

True joy comes of giving of oneself. Those who gain pleasure through bad deeds experience a false sense of gratification and power through the suffering and subjugation of others. This is a fleeting pleasure and only leaves one deeper in the mire of one's own guilt and pain.

True joy is to give without hope of receiving, to love without return. It is by the giving and receiving of love that joy is achieved. Joy is the gift of the divine, only when we can learn to give freely and know the greatness of the gift of life can we fully receive joy.

*The rapture of life... does not arise, unless as perfect music
arises... by the confluence of the mighty and terrific
concords with the subtile(sic) concords. Not by contrast, or
as reciprocal foils, do these elements act... but by union.
They are the sexual forces in music: 'male and female he
created them' and these mighty antagonists do not put forth
their hostilities by repulsion, but by deepest attraction.*
Thomas De Quincy

*If you bring forth what is within you
what you have will save you.
If you do not have that within you,
what you do not have within you will kill you.*
Yeshua Ben Miriam (Jesus of Nazareth)

*O let us live in joy, although having nothing!
In joy let us live like spirits of light!*
Gautama Siddhartha (Buddha)

The Nature of Matter

The natural world is like a calm lake. Its surface appears perfectly flat and in balance or harmony with all around it. But look more closely and see that it is in constant motion, and beneath its surface unknown chaotic forces are at work.

So it is with all matter, the greater harmony and equilibrium of the manifest universe is paradoxically upheld by change, discord, chaos and constant death and rebirth.

The visible world is a symbol of the invisible world.
Jakob Böhme

Light is born of darkness.
Forms are born of the undifferentiated.
The universal Self
That is expressed in all particular selves
is born of Tao.
Lao Tzu

Everything that we see is a shadow cast
by that which we do not see.
Martin Luther King Jr.

The Material Body

Some would have you believe that the apparent world and even our own flesh is inherently bad and a corruption of the divine. If our wine turns to vinegar what profit is to be gained by blaming the glass that holds it? We should not blame our bodies for being a conduit of the senses; nor should we blame the body for what the heart and mind choose for it to do, for surely without the mind to direct it, it is as useless as a boat without a rudder.

All things are created in balance, light and dark, order and chaos, male and female, spirit and flesh. The universe flourishes and propagates itself through the continually shifting balance between polar opposites, that is the nature of all living things and of the universe itself.

If you think you can have good without evil.
right without wrong, order without chaos,
you understand nothing about the laws of the universe.
You cannot have Heaven without Earth.
Yin and Yang only exist together.
Chang Tzu

Neither nakedness, nor entangled hair, nor uncleanliness,
nor fasting, nor sleeping on the ground,
nor covering the body with ashes, nor ever-squatting,
can purify a man who is not pure from doubts and desires.
Gautama Siddhartha (Buddha)

Civilisation

No-one knows how many civilisations have risen and fallen, but like all things they have a beginning and an end. Who knows what treasures have been lost to mankind down the ages? Some nine thousand years before the time of Jesus of Nazareth the sea rose rapidly carrying untold civilisations beneath its waves. Even now the remnants of great cities lie hidden off the coastlines of every continent. Perhaps what Plato wrote of Atlantis was a metaphor for this great loss, men have searched for Atlantis since his time and none have found it.

We should not be overly concerned by the loss or gain of worldly knowledge. What has been gained by mankind has been lost and regained, probably many times over millennia: if a man casts a coin into a pond it becomes lost to him, but surely if the coin remains, could it not be found once more?

*Trying to understand is like straining
to see through muddy water.
Be still and allow the mud to settle.*
Lao Tzu

*As Long as heaven and earth endure, not one letter,
not a single jot of the Law will disappear.*
Yeshua Ben Miriam (Jesus of Nazareth)

*Nature is always like itself,
so that you will not hope
for that which cannot be won
and nothing will remain hidden from you.*
Pythagoras

Good and Evil

Good and evil co-exist as do night and day, one cannot exist without the other. No man is born entirely good or entirely evil.

All of sound mind have the power to choose their actions; surely in our hearts do we not know the difference between the two? Knowing this, it remains only to choose which path to take.

May you be wakeful for learning by us
Those two spirits who are twins
talked among themselves
In thoughts in words and in deeds,
these two spirits are in this way better and worse.
Those who are possessed of good understanding chose truth
but those of wicked understanding did not do so.
Zarathushtra (Zoroaster)

One foot may lead us to an evil way,
the other foot may lead us to a good.
So are all things two, all two.
Letakots-Lesa, Pawnee Chief

The good and evil that are in man's heart
The joy and sorrow that are our fortune and destiny,
Do not impute them to the wheel because
in the light of reason,
The wheel is a thousand times more helpless than you.
Omar Khayyam

Karma

The concept of karma is almost universal.

The idea that you reap what you sow is common to all the major religions of the world. At times it may seem that wrongdoers prosper and that they do not receive what they deserve; likewise the good and just often suffer greatly.

The fruits of one's actions are not always apparent. However, even the most hardened of souls carries the weight of their deeds inside them, throughout life and into the beyond.

Perfect mindedness is thine.
Thine is the wisdom divine of creating the world.
O Ahura Mazda. Thou hast fixed the path
(of awarding due reward) to him who passes his life with
industry and one who is not industrious or idle.
Zarathushtra (Zoroaster)

We were taught to believe that the Great Spirit
sees and hears everything,
and that he never forgets; that hereafter he will give
every man a spirit home according to his deserts.
Hinmatom Yalalkit, Nez Percé Chief

The wrong action seems sweet to the fool
until the reaction comes and brings pain,
and the bitter fruits of wrong deeds
have then to be eaten by the fool.
Gautama Siddhartha (Buddha)

What is sown – love or anger or bitterness:
that shall be your bread.
From The Egyptian Book of the Dead

The End of Everything

One day the world will come to an end as do all things. When this will come to pass is unknown, many have predicted the end of the Earth yet it spins on regardless.

Some believe the universe will collapse in on itself, returning to a state of pure energy before manifesting once more. Others believe in an apocalypse, the end of time, the end of all creation or a day of judgment. No-one can be sure of what will befall God's creation at its end, all we can be sure of is that it must end at some point.

Is it not best to spend one's energy in living well? The end will come without doubt, surely we do not need to know the manner of its coming?

When the sky is rent asunder; when the stars scatter
and the oceans roll together; when the graves are
hurled about; each soul shall know
what it has done and what it has failed to do.
Muhammad

The glorious chariots of kings wear out,
and the body wears out and grows old;
but the virtue of the good never grows old,
and thus they can teach the good to those who are good.
Gautama Siddhartha (Buddha)

Part ii

Master & Pupil

A master set before his pupil five glasses of water:
'Take one, drink from it and be renewed.'
The pupil looked at the glasses and back to his master:
'Which one shall I take master?'
And the master replied:
'It is of no consequence,
for are they not all clean vessels?
'Is not the water within drawn from the same well?'

The Master and Pupil

Until recent generations the wisdom gained with age was given due respect. It is the fashion now to seek immediate resolution to all things. However, knowledge, wisdom and understanding are not subject to rules or to mankind's need for immediate gratification.

Across the world, in all religions, and in most disciplines known to mankind the acolyte learned from his or her master until they too achieved mastery and took on pupils of their own, thus continuing the process in a never-ending cycle.

The great strength of such a system is that, regardless of doctrine, the essence of our experiences of life can pass from one to another in a way that no book alone can achieve. It is true that the pupil can become blinded by seeing the master as some kind of guru and in the case of the corrupt master, who is a charlatan, the pupils become indoctrinated and mere servants to the master's will.

In the purest sense of the master-pupil relationship, the master aids the pupil to teach himself and indeed the master might even learn a thing or two from the pupil.

In the world that we live in where do we go to find a true master? How many truly wish to take on that role? Here the imaginary master is of the universal religion and subscribes to no doctrine that is written down and the pupil asks only questions that transcend the religious divide. I have formulated this part of the book in this way hoping to impart some of what others have taught me and also give answers to what one might consider universal questions, by drawing from the pool of knowledge provided by all the religions of the world.

How can there be a God when so many
people have different beliefs?
Surely not everyone can be right?

God is not judgmental, God does not misunderstand
or mislead. It is mankind that contradicts and
misinterprets, as someone once said – to err is to be
human. Most of us have so little understanding of our
own existence, how can we expect to fully understand
the nature of the universe?

If one looks beyond the corruptions and the doctrines
dictated by man, to the mystical path at the core of all
religions, one can see that they all lead to the same
source. What all the religions point to is that the answers
are right in front of our faces if we only have eyes to
see them. If we can only learn to plumb the depths of
our own hearts that is all we need to do, for God is
everywhere and in everything that ever existed.

The Great Spirit is in all things;
he is in the air we breathe.
The Great Spirit is our Father,
but the earth is our Mother.
She nourishes us, that which we put
into the ground she returns to us.
Bedagi, Wahanaki Alganquin

Three things which from which never to be moved,
one's Oaths, one's Gods and the Truth.
Celtic Triad

How Should I Pray?

Pray with your heart, your mind and your soul.

Let no man tell you how to pray for you alone can find your own path to God.

Do not waste your time in praying for bad things, for you will ultimately visit harm upon yourself.

Praise the name of your Lord, the Most High,
who has created all things and proportioned them;
who has ordained their destinies and guided them;
who brings forth the green pastures,
then turns it to withered grass?
Muhammad

My Mother taught...
me to kneel and pray to Usen for strength,
health, wisdom and protection.
We never prayed against any individual,
we ourselves took vengeance.
We were taught that Usen does not care
for the petty quarrels of men.
Goyathlay, Chiricahua Apache Chief

Each one prays to God according to his own light.
Mohandas Karamchand Gandhi

Is It Wrong To Want Possessions?

We must know that possessions have only a small importance within our lives. Jesus of Nazareth said: 'People cannot live on bread alone', and Buddha spoke often of the foolishness of pursuing material wealth.

All men need to live, to eat and be sustained in life, but when all our physical needs are met, what more do we need of the world?

What we acquire in our lifetimes cannot be taken beyond the point of our death, our material greed only serves to deprive others of what they need – enough is as good as a feast.

Wealth destroys the fool who seeks not the Beyond.
Because of greed for wealth
the fool destroys himself as if he were his own enemy.
Gautama Siddhartha (Buddha)

Men love what they may grasp in their hands,
Yet they do not love the ground that supports their weight.
Anon

Fortunate are you who are poor,
for yours is the realm of God.
Yeshua Ben Miriam (Jesus of Nazareth)

Riches would do us no good.
We could not take them with us to the other world.
We do not want riches, we want peace and love.
Makhpiya-Luta, Sioux Chief

Is It Foolish To Believe In The Supernatural?

Just because these things are unproven by science it does not mean that they are false. Less than 200 years ago man had no concept of radio waves, X-rays or television signals.

If these things are accepted as part of everyday life even though we cannot see or feel them, why should we reject the supernatural simply because it cannot be seen by the majority?

There is a whole vista of creation invisible to the human eyes, which we are only beginning to discover; God's creation has not changed, it is merely our perception of it that has changed.

Those who realise Me as existing in the physical plane,
the divine planes...
have a mind which is focused and know Me
even at the time of death.
From The Bhagavad-Gítá

There is nothing hidden except to be made visible;
nothing is secret except to come to light.
Yeshua Ben Miriam (Jesus of Nazareth)

What Is The Third Eye?

The third eye is known by many names, to some as the inner eye, inner vision, second sight, enlightenment etc. This concept is common to a great many religions and spiritual paths around the world.

It is the ability to see beyond our own limited perception of existence and catch a glimpse of how things really are.

His disciples said to him
'When will the kingdom come?'
It will not come by watching for it.
It will not be said 'Look here' or 'Look there!',
Rather the Father's kingdom is spread out
upon the earth and people don't see it.
From The Gospel of Doubting Thomas

The man who sat on the ground in his tipi
meditating on life and its meaning,
accepting the kinship of all creatures,
and acknowledging unity
with the universe of things,
was infusing into his being
the true essence of civilisation.
Standing Bear, Oglala Sioux Chief

How Do I Open My Third Eye?

There is no correct answer to this question; it is different for every person. However, there are tools that man has used to aid him in that task. For most it is by finding the stillness in your soul that moments of enlightenment come – achieving that is the difficulty. Meditation is a practice common to all religions of the world which can be greatly effective in this task.

Paradoxically we must learn to truly listen to all our senses, but at the same time learn how to switch them off, so that we can pursue the inner journey without distraction.

For most enlightenment is not a flash or thunderbolt that changes one forever, it is a fleeting moment of connection to the divine. Just as our eyes do, the third eye can close as well as open.

Blessed are the eyes that see what you see.
For I say to you many prophets and kings
desired to see what you see but did not see it,
and to hear what you hear, but did not hear it.
Yeshua Ben Miriam (Jesus of Nazareth)

Teachers open the door, but you must enter by yourself.
Chinese proverb

He who's soul is satisfied
with the wisdom of spiritual knowledge,
who has attained complete control
over his senses and is unshakeable,
to whom a lump of earth, a stone and gold are the same,
such a yogi is said to have attained realisation.
From The Bhagavad-Gítá

How Did The World Begin?

Every religion has a creation myth, and that is exactly what they are – myths, a symbolic account of creation, not to be taken literally, although many have made that mistake. Even now scientists cannot be entirely sure of the origins of the universe and they will never know what caused it to come into being.

What we can be fairly certain of is how the earth and our solar system was created. The earth and all the planets were formed from fragments of the swirling mass that became our sun. It is from this source that all living creatures originate and that same source sustains life on this planet. The earliest known cultures knew the importance of the sun and worshiped it as the giver of light and life, it is indeed the source of the world and all life upon it.

The divine Surya is the refuge
or home of innumerable wonders.
All the creatures that inhabit the three worlds
have flowed from Surya.
From The Mahabharata

Praise be to God, Creator of Heaven and Earth!
...He multiplies His creatures according to His will.
God has power over all things.
Muhammad

Who smootheth the ruggedness of a mountain?
Who is He who announceth the ages of the moon?
And who, the place where falleth the sunset?
From The Song of Amergin

What Is The Greatest Secret Of The Universe?

The greatest secret is that there are no secrets; everything we need to know is already revealed to us. If we fail to perceive this truth that is because we simply do not see what is right under our noses.

Three candles that illuminate every darkness:
Truth, Nature and Knowledge.
Celtic Triad

Preoccupied with the quest to learn
what they do not naturally know,
men lose the intuitive knowledge
they already naturally possess.
Chang Tzu

All the religions of the world, while they may differ
in other respects, unitedly proclaim that nothing lives in
this world but Truth.
Mohandas Karamchand Gandhi

What Is Love?

Love is a much used and often abused term. Some never know love, some cannot give love and other cannot receive it, but in our hearts we all understand what love is.

To truly love another is to touch the divine, it is beyond description; when we love we create something truly beautiful.

Love is patient; love is kind;
love is not envious or boastful or arrogant or rude.
It does not insist on its own way;
it is not irritable or resentful;
It does not rejoice in wrongdoing, but rejoices in the truth.
It bears all things, believes all things, hopes all things,
endures all things.
Saul of Tarsus (St. Paul)

The wise aren't full of themselves,
the more they do for others,
the more they feel fulfilled.
The more they give to others,
the more they feel they have.
Lao Tzu

Do you not wish God to forgive you?
God is forgiving and merciful.
Muhammad

Why Is There Suffering In The World?

Mankind brings suffering upon himself. We live in paradise but we turn it to wasteland through our own foul deeds. God does not bring suffering upon us, even natural disasters are part of the cycles of the earth, they are neither caused or prevented by God.

For the most part our sufferings are of our own making or of those around us, and often the pain we bear is passed from one to another until someone is able to break the chain of suffering.

Although there is much unnecessary pain and torment, suffering is not without value, for it teaches us humility, wisdom and the ability to value what gifts life has given us. Many of the most valuable lessons in life are gained through bitter experience – suffer to learn.

I have known many sorrows,
most of which never happened.
Mark Twain

Swans follow the path of the sun
by the miracle of flying through the air.
Men who are strong conquer evil and its armies;
and they rise far above the world.
Gautama Siddhartha (Buddha)

Three things increase wisdom:
Misfortune, Illness, and Enemies.
Celtic Triad

Is There Such A Place As Hell?

The concept of hell has been used down the ages to manipulate the masses, as an instrument of fear and suppression; the traditional image of hell is probably far from reality. Hell is a place of our making and it is not necessary for us to die to visit it. For those who have any understanding of their own deeds, the wickedness they unleash upon the world also accumulates in their own hearts, creating their own private hell.

Even those who appear impervious to any form of retribution are not beyond the all-seeing eye of God; for if they do not pay in this life, the truly evil will surely reap their bitter harvest in the next.

Our destinies lie in our own hands; we have the power to nurture this planet or turn it into a living hell. Likewise, in our individual lives, we can choose a path towards hell or enlightenment; although we may stumble, stray or fall, in our hearts we still know which path we follow.

For the bases of the mountains shall melt
And fire shall consume the deep places of Hell
But thou wilt deliver
All those that are corrected by Thy judgments.
Dead Sea Scroll IQH

Some people are born on this earth,
those who do evil are reborn in hell;
the righteous go to heaven;
but those who are pure reach Nirvana.
Gautama Siddhartha (Buddha)

Oh, would that you knew what the Day of Judgment is!
It is the day when every soul will stand alone
and God will reign supreme.
Muhammad

Should I Fear Death?

Death is part of life, without it the world would be choked. All things have their time and pass away; even the sun, the life of which seems infinite if compared to a human lifetime, will eventually fade and die.

It is the natural order that all things shall decline to make way for the new, we do well to accept the inevitable. Perhaps instead of fearing death, we should fear the waste of what life we have, every day is precious, for one day it will be our last.

Hatred, vengeance and all such things are pathways to death. Death is a necessary part of life – to bring balance. But this energy should never be unchecked, lest it consume our own inner light. This same light of love and life that shines from our hearts shines throughout all of creation. It is our connection to the divine and without it there is only death and darkness.

The night is at hand and it is good to yield to the night.
Homer

There is no death, only a change of worlds.
Seatlh, Suquamish Chief

Death is to life what returning is to going away.
Death is a return to where we set out from
when we were born.
Lin Lei

Self Discipline

By discipline I do not mean austerity and self-harm, I do not believe aesthetic austerity is a necessary means of touching the divine.

To me self discipline is simply a matter of trying to avoid those things that are destructive to us on a physical, emotional and spiritual level. This allows our hearts to be open and give freely, which offers its own rewards.

Be disciplined with
The body and the mind
But be always gentle
With your soul,
For it is as eternal
As the cosmos itself.

Let compassion, generosity,
Passion and love
Be its gifts and
You shall see and hear
All the joys of creation.

Thanksgiving Prayer

I say this prayer every day to remind myself of how wonderful the world is and how lucky and blessed I am. As children we all appreciate the beauty of God's earth. How sad it is that as we grow up we often forgot and lose ourselves in foolish human concerns. For some this happens to the extent that we shut our hearts so that we no longer notice the flowers, the wonder of a sunset or the birds singing.

The whole world is a miraculous blessing; if a child can see this simple truth, then the man or woman who cannot is truly lost. Even so, the lost can be found and the child in all of us, although maybe silenced, can be found again.

I give thanks this day
For the Sun upon the Earth
For the wind through the trees
For the magic of starlight
And the ever-changing moon,
For the rivers that run
To the swelling seas
And for the rich ground
Upon which I stand.

Thanks to G. Mc. for inspiring me.
Thanks to W. K. for advice, having the ear
bent off you and several proof-reads.

Some of the profits of this book will be donated to:
Earth Love Fund
Barnardos
Greenpeace

Also by Luke Eastwood:
The Druid's Primer (Moon Books)
You can read more of his work at lukeeastwood.com

Moon Books invites you to begin or deepen your encounter with Paganism, in all its rich, creative, flourishing forms.